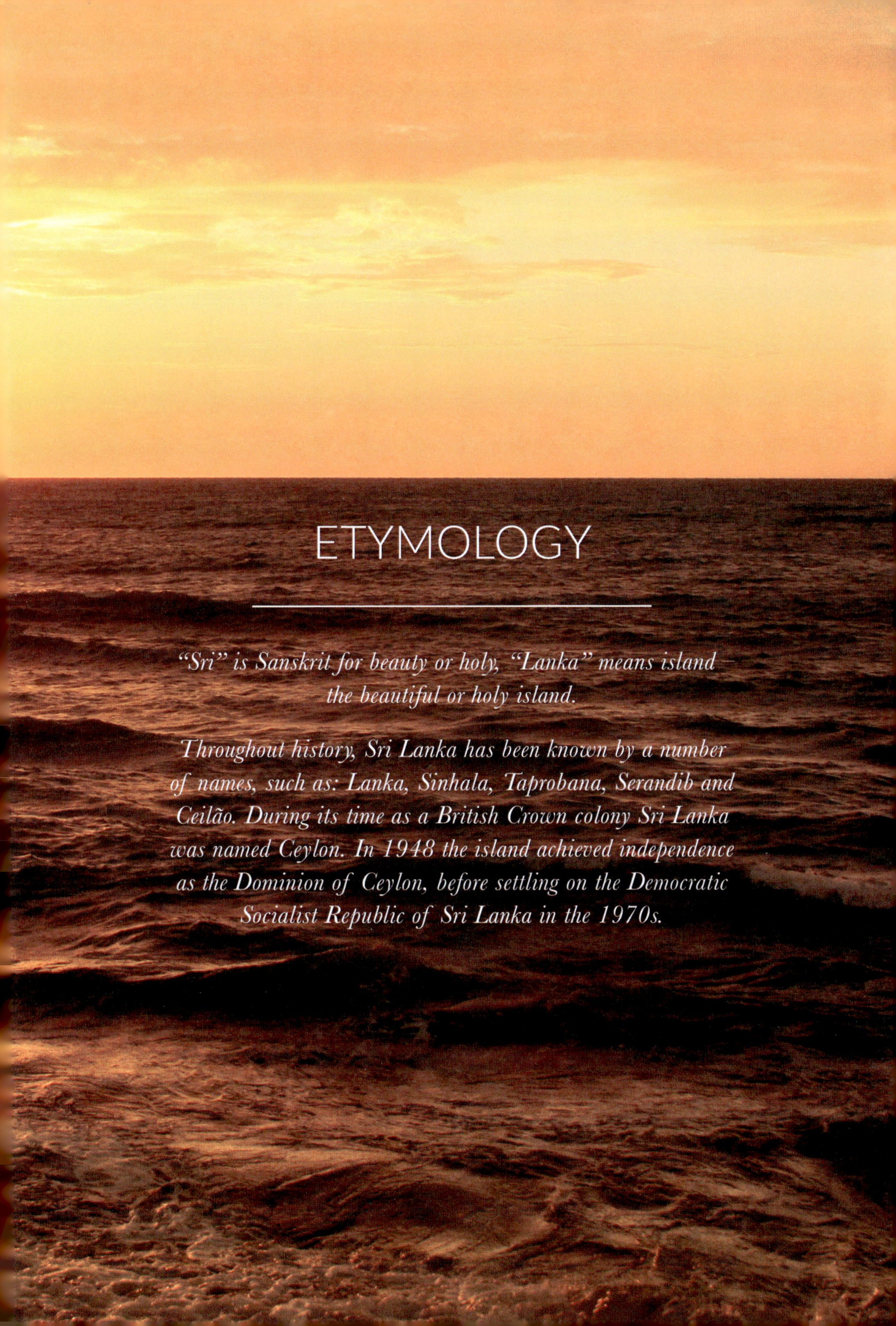

ETYMOLOGY

"Sri" is Sanskrit for beauty or holy, "Lanka" means island – the beautiful or holy island.

Throughout history, Sri Lanka has been known by a number of names, such as: Lanka, Sinhala, Taprobana, Serandib and Ceilão. During its time as a British Crown colony Sri Lanka was named Ceylon. In 1948 the island achieved independence as the Dominion of Ceylon, before settling on the Democratic Socialist Republic of Sri Lanka in the 1970s.

SRI LANKA – PEARL OF THE INDIAN OCEAN

Foreword

Marco Polo, the 13th century Venetian explorer, called Sri Lanka "The most beautiful island in the world."

In this book, I would like to share some of the highlights of my travels and stays in Sri Lanka. What fascinated me most about Sri Lanka is the combined colonial and cultural heritage, the fantastic people and the variety of experiences. From the wildlife and nature, to its illustrious tea heritage and as a melting pot for the world's religions, Sri Lanka really does have something for everyone.

However, it was not so long ago that we had a much darker image of Sri Lanka. It is a country that has endured more than 25 years of civil war and on Boxing Day 2004, the island was struck by a tsunami that claimed over 30,000 lives. When I first came to Sri Lanka in 2011 – just two years after the civil war came to an end and seven years after the tsunami – I did not know what to expect.

Although civil war was still a recent, painful memory, there was a feeling of optimism in the air.

The island was at peace, but the military was still very present, with military ships patrolling the coast. However, for the people of Sri Lanka, the wounds were beginning to heal and it was the beginning of a new era. Peace was welcomed and the optimism for a better future was prevalent. It was a special time to get to know Sri Lanka and to fall in love with the island.

While exploring the island, I started to photograph my path. I took photos to express the feeling, soul and beauty of Sri Lanka. I hope that this book will inspire you to explore the island, experience its wonder and create your own memories and impressions. Sri Lanka is truly a pearl in the Indian Ocean. To visit once may be the beginning of a lifelong addiction.

I wish you happy travels when visiting the most beautiful island in the world.

Lina Nicander

FAST FACTS

- 8 UNESCO World Heritage Sites
- 1,330 kilometres of coastline – much of which is pristine beaches
- 15 national parks
- 500,000 acres of lush tea estates
- 250 acres of botanical gardens
- 350 waterfalls
- 25,000 bodies of water
- A culture dating back to over 2,500 years

Source: Sri Lanka Tourism

22

53

107

39

38
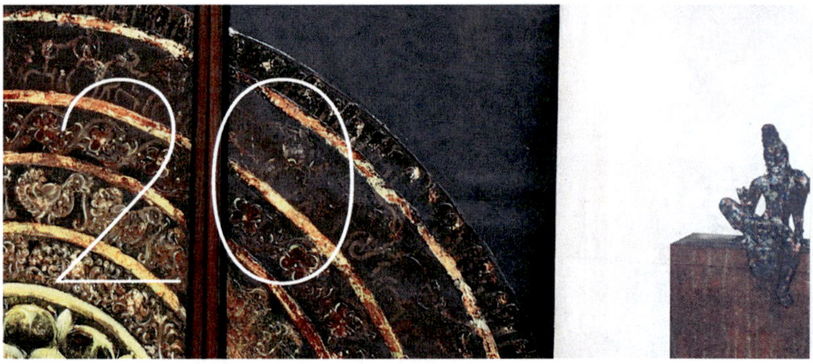
20

78

CONTENTS

EXPLORE THE BEAUTY OF SRI LANKA

Introduction

In this book, we will visit four of the eight sites of the UNESCO world list: The old town of Galle and Galle Fort, the sacred city of Kandy, the ancient city of Sigiriya and the Central Highlands of Sri Lanka. We will also enjoy Ceylon tea, stroll through the Royal Botanical Gardens, take a train journey through the country's scenic landscape and experience Cinnamon Gardens in Colombo on a lush Sunday afternoon. I would also like to introduce you to the architect Geoffrey Bawa, who has influenced Sri Lanka's modern architecture through his beautiful tropical modernism.

COLOMBO

Pink sunrise over Colombo • Take a walk through Cinnamon Gardens • Visit Paradise Road The Gallery Café and discover Geoffrey Bawa • The finest colonial hotels • See the Dutch Museum • Explore Negombo's waterways, beaches and fish markets

GOOD MORNING COLOMBO

The city awakes

The pink sunrise over Colombo marks what is possibly the most beautiful moment of the day. As the sun rises over the horizon it spreads a beautiful pink light over the capital and the morning mist dissolves, revealing a city gearing up to its fast daily pace. Along the river banks, the birds' dawn chorus is almost deafening. To experience the exotic nature during these moments is, in itself, worth the trip to Sri Lanka.

Kumar the Buddhist tuk-tuk driver lights an incense stick on the front of his vehicle, picks up the kids to take them to school and morning in Colombo begins.

COLO

SIGHTSEEING IN THE CAPITAL

Street life

Colombo is the metropolitan area of Sri Lanka, with more than 6 million people living here. The city itself has a population of around 800,000 people. This busy, vibrant, coastal city boasts lots of green spaces and a mixture of modern life, with new built high-rise buildings that coalesce with old colonial buildings and the traditional Sri Lankan way of life.

As you take the Galle Road which follows the coastline from Mount Lavinia up to Colombo Fort, it is hard to get your head around Colombo. The city, and Sri Lanka in general, is filled with traffic. TATA buses blow out black fumes, while the tuk-tuks, motorcycles and cars dodge the crossing pedestrians and cyclists. Meanwhile, dogs lay lazily in the middle of street without a care. All these contribute to the higgledy-piggledy, coordinated rhythm of Colombo street life, that only people who know how to drive in this city can understand and navigate.

Travelling around Colombo during rush hours, such as when school starts or ends between 1–2 PM, or when people return home from work, can take a long time. Planning your route in advance is important to avoid getting stuck in traffic. Call and schedule taxis and vans ahead of departure.

The best day to visit the capital is Sunday as many of Colombo's inhabitants leave for the weekend. They retreat to second homes, visit their families or head to the highlands or the south coast beaches to escape the heat. This gives you the perfect opportunity to take a tuk-tuk through the lush, empty avenues in Cinnamon Gardens or along Galle Face, to see the Indian Ocean and feel the wind in your hair.

BAR
Coca-Cola
BEER BAR
Wattala.
MANJULA RESTURANT & BEER BAR
Coca-Cola
Coca-Cola
QX - 7506
RE

CINNAMON GARDENS – A COLONIAL WALK

Cinnamon Gardens is an exclusive neighbourhood in the Colombo 07 district. Its beautiful name originates from the cinnamon plantations that grew here historically. Today it is home to colonial villas and buildings, foreign embassies, international schools and prominent buildings such as Colombo Town Hall and the National Museum.

This verdant neighbourhood is filled with big, old banyan trees and boasts the city's oldest and largest park, Viharamahadevi Park.

Did you know?

Most of the world's cinnamon comes from Sri Lanka. It is produced from the bark of the cinnamon tree. These trees once grew wild in Sri Lanka, but today cinnamon is cultivated agriculturally on cinnamon plantations.

A STROLL IN THE PARK

Viharamahadevi Park, Colombo 07

Viharamahadevi Park is the largest and oldest park in Colombo. Originally named Victoria Park, it was named after Britain's Queen Victoria. Following Sri Lanka's independence, in the 1950s the park changed its name to Viharamahadevi Park, named after one of Sri Lanka's greatest heroines and mother of the Sinhalese King Dutugamunu, Queen Viharamahadevi.

There's lots to do in Viharamahadevi Park. It's a wonderful place to take a stroll and there is a large children's playground that is usually buzzing with activity. Pass by the golden Buddha and take a look at the Town Hall, which resembles the US Capitol.

OUTDOOR ART MARKET

Kala Pola Art Market, Ananda Coomaraswamy Mawatha, Colombo 07

Head south of the park and on Sunday mornings you will find Kala Pola Art Market. Here the local artists meet to sell their works. Like the artistic styles and motives, the quality of the paintings differs, but it is a great place to pick up a piece of local art.

Open: Sundays, 8 AM–12 noon.

COLOMBO NATIONAL MUSEUM

Sir Marcus Fernando Mawatha, Colombo 07

With its slumbering charm, Colombo National Museum is a bit like a British museum from the turn of the century.

Founded in 1877, the museum is protected by the long, lingering vines of a large, old banyan tree. Judging by its impressive root system and the vines that hang from it, I wouldn't be surprised if it was as old as the museum. The building's architecture harks back to the country's British colonial era.

Here you can learn about Sri Lanka's cultural and natural heritage, discover beautiful traditional crafts and see the impressive 17th century throne made for King Wimaladharmasuriya, along with the crown jewels of Kandy's monarchs.

Colombo Racecourse in Colombo's Cinnamon Gardens neighbourhood.

A DAY AT THE RACES

Colombo Racecourse, Reid Avenue, Colombo 07

Once an important event on the social calendar, historically Colombo racecourse was filled with elegant ladies dressed in long, white flowing dresses and beautiful hats and jockeys in their colourful silks. Today it is the home of Sri Lanka's first international grade Rugby Union ground and Colombo Racecourse shopping mall.

Colombo Racecourse began as a racecourse for harness racing in 1893. During World War II it was used as a temporary airfield for the Royal Air Force (RAF). Following its decline, in 2012 it was redeveloped and reopened as Colombo Racecourse Sports Complex. Two years later, the beautiful white colonial Racecourse Promenade was also converted into a mall filled with shops and restaurants.

LAW & ORDER

Cinnamon Gardens Police Station,
42 Premasiri Khemadasa Mawatha, Colombo 07

Built in the late 1800s, Cinnamon Gardens Police Station is still in operation. It bears all the classic characteristics of a colonial police station, such as high ceilings and large windows.

TIME FOR TEA (OR COFFEE)

The Coffee Bean & Tea Leaf, 2 Maitland Crescent, Colombo 07

After a long, hot walk through Cinnamon Gardens, it's nice to stop and grab a cup of strong coffee or Sri Lanka's national drink – tea. Part of a café chain, The Coffee Bean & Tea Leaf also offers Wi-Fi and a blueberry cheesecake that is to die for.

FASHIONABLE COLOMBO

Arcade - Independence Square, Colombo 07

Built in 1889, one of Sri Lanka's latest retail landmarks, Arcade – Independence Square was originally a psychiatric hospital. The arcade was completely renovated in 2012 and is now filled with a host of shops and restaurants, including Tsukiji Uoichi, a Japanese restaurant that is popular among both Sri Lankans and Japanese business people in Colombo.

The Arcade is close to many of the schools in Cinnamon Gardens, making it a popular hangout for the city's teenagers. Its exterior also serves as a popular backdrop for wedding portraits.

THE FINEST COLONIAL HOTELS

Combining old world hospitality and colonial style with breathtaking views of the Indian Ocean, Colombo's beachfront hotels are the perfect place to relax and recharge the batteries.

GALLE FACE HOTEL – A UNIQUE HOTEL WITH A FAMOUS HISTORY

2 Galle Road, Colombo 03

Built in 1864 by British entrepreneurs, this is one of the oldest hotels in Sri Lanka. Many famous names have passed through the reception of the Galle Face Hotel, and there's even a little exhibition of all the prominent guests who have stayed here. Mahatma Gandhi, Emperor Hirohito of Japan, Queen Elizabeth II, Sir Laurence Olivier and the writer George Bernard Shaw are just a few. A local celebrity and something of an institution was the hotel's famous doorman, Kottarapattu Chattu Kuttan, who took care of guests for 72 years. He joined the hotel as a waiter in 1942 and later became the welcoming face of the hotel as its doorman. He continued working until just a few months before his death in 2014 at the age of 94. Upon the news of his death the BBC wrote an article about him and his life.

The hotel has a nice, friendly atmosphere, with a well-kept interior and a lovely pool area which offers the perfect vantage point for taking in the unforgettable view of the sun setting over the Indian Ocean. The hotel is also just a short walk from Galle Face Green, an ocean-side promenade and public park which runs along Galle Road and stretches for a half kilometre along the coast. Alternatively, you can take a tuk-tuk to visit Colombo Fort or Cinnamon Gardens, which are only 10 minutes away.

MOUNT LAVINIA HOTEL – COLONIAL HERITAGE

100 Hotel Road, Mount Lavinia

A bit further down south along the Galle Road is the Mount Lavinia Hotel. Also in the colonial style, the hotel is one of Sri Lanka's oldest hotels. Built in 1806 as a residence for Sir Thomas Maitland, the second Governor of British Ceylon, the colonial mansion is a popular destination for visitors to Sri Lanka either at the beginning or end of their holiday.

Like the Galle Face Hotel, here you can experience breathtaking sunset views over the Indian Ocean, and since the hotel is set on a promontory, it offers fantastic views of the Colombo coastline. Mount Lavinia Hotel can be seen from the train as it passes by along Sri Lanka's coastal line – the country's second railway line – which was constructed by the government in 1877.

Its location offers a lovely coastal breeze in the afternoon, so there's nothing better than relaxing by the pool on a hot Colombo afternoon. Even if you're not a resident, it is possible to buy a pool ticket.

TROPICAL MODERNISM

A splendid fusion

In Sri Lanka, tropical modernism incorporates a splendid fusion of indigenous Sinhalese style, Dutch colonial influence and European modernism, in harmony with the natural surroundings. Sri Lanka's most famous architect, Geoffrey Bawa, is best known as the country's founding father of tropical modernism.

The 20th century architectural style stems from modernist architecture. Inspired by architects such as Le Corbusier and Fry and Drew, tropical modernism is rooted in the warm, tropical climates of Africa, Asia and South America. Based on the qualities and essential concepts of modernism, the architectural style incorporates the use of local construction materials and building traditions, combined with an emphasis on quality, simplicity, sustainability and most notably, a respect for nature.

GEOFFREY BAWA

Tropical Modernist

Geoffrey Bawa (1919-2003), is Sri Lanka's most celebrated architect and one of the most influential Asian architects of the 20th century. He is best known as an early proponent of tropical modernism.

Born into a British-Ceylon family, Geoffrey Bawa was educated as a lawyer at Cambridge University in England. It was not until he was 38 years old and had been living in Italy that he began working with architecture. He returned to Sri Lanka and began his career as an architect, a profession in which he became world-renowned. His work has influenced the design concept of almost every newly built hotel in Sri Lanka.

In the early days, Bawa worked together with the Danish Architect Ulrik Plesner, who became a partner of the architect's Colombo studio. Bawa's most famous projects include Sri Lanka's Parliament Building in Kotte (1982) and hotels such as: Jetwing Lighthouse in Galle, Club Villa in Bentota and The Blue Water Hotel and Spa in Wadduwa.

The success of Bawa's design concept is down to buildings which are restful and open, blending seamlessly with nature. Bawa balanced a combination of materials such as terracotta tiles, concrete and wood, with nature, which he then merged with Asian traditions, colonial heritage and European modernism. His style was inspired by Dutch colonial villas and traditional Sinhalese Walauwas with their open-sided rooms, large courtyards and spacious verandas.

PARADISE ROAD THE GALLERY CAFÉ

The former office of architect Geoffrey Bawa
2 Alfred House Rd, Colombo 03

This was once the office of Geoffrey Bawa. Established in 1998, Paradise Road The Gallery Café holds exhibitions of contemporary artists from Sri Lanka and South Asia, which change each month. The café has a beautiful courtyard and the entire building is filled with the spirit of Geoffrey Bawa – from the design of the restaurant to the style of the rest-rooms. The beauty of Asian modernism was Bawa's signature style and has become a part of the Paradise Road Group's brand concept and identity.

Enjoy lunch, dinner or just relax for a while and take a look at the exhibition.

THE BLUE WATER HOTEL AND SPA, WADDUWA

Thalpitiya, Wadduwa

Designed by Geoffrey Bawa in the 1990s, this five-star hotel was one of Bawa's last projects. Here you can experience his minimalist style through his use of space, terracotta and frangipani trees.

COLOMBO FORT

York and Church Street, Colombo 01

Let's go to Colombo Fort and take a stroll around the old area, which is the city's central business and financial district. Nowadays it is much sleepier than I imagine it was during its colonial heyday, but it really is worth visiting and taking a walk around Colombo's oldest area.

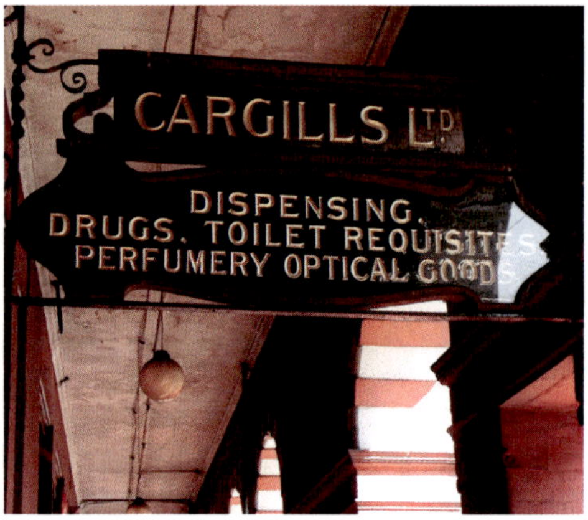

COLOMBO'S HISTORIC QUARTER

The Fort district

A visit to Colombo Fort is a must. The city's main railway station is situated here, in the heart of Colombo. Here you can find many examples of colonial architecture and Sri Lanka's heritage. The centre of colonial Colombo is the Fort district. Starting at the iconic Cargills building, there are many interesting buildings to see.

It can get quite hot around Colombo Fort, so after a while it can be rewarding to take a break at the air conditioned t-Lounge by Dilmah.

CARGILLS BUILDING – A DEPARTMENT STORE WITH HISTORY

York St, Colombo 01

This beautiful building, with its original Cargills sign is eye-catching and remains a unique sight in Colombo. From the outside it seems dark and uninhabited, but inside the original wooden interior is still to be seen. It is almost like a museum of a department store from the early 20th century. On the ground floor, the curious old statue of 'Goddess Minerva', which stood on the gable of the old Governor's house, still stands, in top condition.

Looking at the old signs that still hang on the exterior, it is easy to imagine how Cargills was once a buzzing, vibrant commercial centre, popular with the Europeans of Colombo at the beginning of the 20th century. Today, Cargills (Ceylon) PLC is a well-established Sri Lankan retail, food and restaurant chain and bank.

COLOMBO GENERAL POST OFFICE (1895)

Kings St, Colombo 01

Entering Colombo's General Post Office building in Colombo Fort is like entering the Titanic. This Edwardian style building is very impressive. At the end of the 19th century, post offices were considered as important and high tech as the telecom and computer giants are today and this post office can be compared to the Apple concept stores in major cities.

CENTRAL POINT – THE ECONOMIC HISTORY MUSEUM OF SRI LANKA

Chatham St, Colombo 01

Formerly the National Mutual Life Association of Australia, the restored neo-classical style building, which was the tallest in Colombo when it was built in 1914, is now the home of Sri Lanka's Economic History Museum.

T-LOUNGE BY DILMAH

Chatham St, Colombo 01

The t-Lounge by Dilmah is just what you need to recharge the batteries after walking around the Colombo Fort in the heat. Here you can enjoy freshly brewed Ceylon tea or a cool iced tea and a selection of delicious cakes, crepes and sandwiches. You can also buy some of Dilmah's famous tea varieties here to take home, such as Prince of Kandy, Nuwara Eliya Pekoe, green tea with jasmine or pure chamomile.

t
LOUNGE
ON CHATHAM STREET
BY
Dilmah
Tea of the Month

EVENING AT THE DUTCH HOSPITAL

Hospital St, Colombo 01

One of the oldest buildings in Colombo Fort, this former hospital was built by the Dutch in 1681. It served the staff of the Dutch East India Company, as well as Dutch seafarers. In 2011, the Dutch Hospital building was converted into a lively shopping precinct with restaurants, but the historic architecture of the building remains well preserved. The best times to visit are lunchtime and evenings, when it is buzzing with life.

MINISTRY OF CRAB

4 Old Dutch Hospital, Colombo 01

A standout restaurant at the Dutch Hospital is The Ministry of Crab, a modern celebration of Sri Lanka's lagoon crab, which is fished in Negombo and served in a number of creative ways. The restaurant is very popular, so be sure to book a table in advance.

It is a fantastic feeling to climb the old stairs of robust wood and enter the courtyard. The house is surrounded by new buildings, so there is a real feeling of how close the building was to being demolished.

Within the preserved colonial atmosphere, the museum holds a collection of items related to the country's Dutch legacy, from furniture, glass and ceramics, to weapons, maps and even tombstones.

THE DUTCH MUSEUM – A HIDDEN GEM

95 Prince Street, Colombo 01

The Dutch Museum is a treasure hidden within the busy Pettah district. Pettah is a multi-ethnic neighbourhood that is intense, vibrant and busy with trade. The old lanes are narrow and it is easy to get lost. The museum can be hard to find, but just ask someone in the street and they will be happy to help.

The museum building is over 300 years old and has the architectural features of a colonial Dutch townhouse. It was the official residence of Thomas van Rhee, the Dutch Governor of Sri Lanka between 1692–1697. In the 1970s in a state of severe disrepair, the building was saved and restored with financial support from the Government of the Netherlands. Following extensive restoration, the museum opened in 1982.

GREEN COLOMBO

Colombo is a city undergoing fast urban development. It has lots of green spaces and this makes the city very special. I hope that Colombo will develop with sustainability in mind, as it will be to the city's advantage in the future to retain its untouched natural areas filled with nature along the rivers and canals, rather than to fall for the temptation of building new high-rise tower blocks. Colombo's main challenge now is its transport network. The increasing daily traffic jams highlight the need for better public transport and bicycle lanes would allow people to travel by cycle in Colombo safely.

In the Colombo suburbs of Rajagiriya and Sri Jayawardenepura in Kotte, you can experience the city's rich birdlife. The abundance of nature in the urban forests, as well as the areas' wetlands and fresh water bodies provide the perfect habitats for a diverse variety of species.

NEGOMBO

Close to Colombo

Negombo is a city with a colonial heritage. Situated just 37 km from Colombo and even closer to Bandaranaike International Airport, it is easily accessed via the highway. Its accessible location and beach has made it a popular destination for tourists, particularly as they begin or end their journey.

Negombo is also popular among expats and natives of Colombo as a weekend destination. Many take a Sunday excursion to spend the day at the pool or to enjoy a game of cricket and dinner.

It's wonderful to enjoy high tea with freshly brewed Ceylon tea served on the beach in the shade of the banyan and palm trees, watching the children play and the catamaran boats sail in and out.

LITTLE ROME

In Negombo there are many traces of Sri Lanka's colonial legacy. The Portuguese who came in the 15th and 16th century were Catholics and many Sri Lankans converted to Catholicism. Here you will meet many Sri Lankans with the surname "Fernando" or "Fernandez".

In Negombo, two-thirds of the population are Roman Catholic, the rest being mainly Buddhists, Hindus and Muslims. For this reason, the city is also known as "Little Rome".

Wild cinnamon plays an important role in Negombo's history. The Portuguese held control over cinnamon production over a period of 100 years. In the ensuing power struggle between the Portuguese and the Kingdom of Kandy, the King of Kandy turned to the Dutch, who in turn, captured Negombo from the Portuguese. The Dutch built Negombo Fort in 1672 and improved the city's canal system. Following a British takeover in 1815, Negombo lost its strategic role and became a fishing and seafood hub. In 1907 it became connected through the British controlled railway project, which provided efficient transportation, thus opening up new possibilities.

CATCH OF THE DAY – NEGOMBO FISH MARKET

Mankuliya Road, Negombo

This is a fantastic world of busy trade and many different types of fish. It is smelly, intense and you will be amazed by the immense supply of seafood. The daily catch is both from the open sea and Negombo Lagoon where lobsters, crabs and prawns are found. Deep sea fishing provides the market with an impressive variety of swordfish, tuna, squid, shark and more. Many of the city's more upmarket restaurants, such as Ministry of Crab in the Dutch Hospital, serve fish and seafood freshly caught in Negombo that morning.

The fish market is open every day except Sundays, from 5 AM. The best time to visit is early morning.

BEAUTIFUL BATIK SAILS OF THE ORUWA

Catamarans, also known as Oruwa are the traditional Sri Lankan sailing vessels and are typical for the Negombo region. Used by the local fishermen, they have beautiful sun-kissed batik sails, which complement the ochre coloured sand of the beaches of the Negombo and Colombo regions, which is darker and more coarse than the fine white sand of the south coast.

EXPLORING THE WATERWAYS

The Dutch Canal in Negombo is a part of the 14.5 km Hamilton Canal, which connects Puttalam in the north with Colombo. The canal is part of Sri Lanka's history and a legacy of the Dutch, who contributed with their expertise. It is amazing to see how straight the Dutch canal is. When the British came, rail became the main method of transportation, but the canal is still in use and a lot of houses and developments are built close to the canals.

The history of the canals dates back to the 15th century when the King of Kotte, Veera Parakramabahu, had a network of canals built to enable the transportation of cardamom, pepper and cinnamon. It is possible to take a tour of the Dutch canal, which enters the Negombo Lagoon. The waterways are worth exploring both for their nature and from a historical standpoint.

NEGOMBO STATION – TRAVEL BACK IN TIME

Take the train from Negombo to Colombo Fort railway station, as it is a lovely and inexpensive experience. It's also a good way to meet the people of Sri Lanka and get a taste of daily life. The trip offers beautiful tropical scenery, while the wagon's open doors provide a lovely breeze. However, avoid the rush hours when the train is packed full of commuters going to work in Colombo or back home to Negombo.

Negombo railway station opened in 1909 and is the 24th station on the Puttalam line from Colombo Fort. With its calm green walls and huge ceiling fan, Negombo railway station is a bit like walking onto the set of the classic British TV series *The Jewel in the Crown*.

NORTH OF COLOMBO

Take the train from Colombo to Kandy • Visit the beautiful Botanical Gardens • Temple of the Tooth • A walk by Kandy Lake • High tea at Queen's Hotel

SCENIC VIEWS BY RAIL

The morning train to Kandy

Once you leave the railway station in Colombo, you see village life from the train window as you pass by, on the way to Kandy. The houses, small gardens, clothes hanging out to dry, children playing, an elderly man cycling - all bathed in the golden morning light.

After Colombo the train starts moving uphill and more scenic views flash by your window, from tea plantations to tropical jungles. It is so beautiful that you may feel the urge to jump off the train and start a new life right there.

If you book in advance you can choose to travel in a specific wagon. The Observation Saloon is the last wagon on the train, with a big window that offers great views of the tracks and landscape. To travel in the Observation Saloon, it is necessary to reserve in advance through the Sri Lanka Railway Department.

railway.gov.lk

Kandy surrounds the beautiful Kandy lake. It is nice to take a walk around the lake, passing by the Temple of the Tooth, followed by a visit to the colonial Queen's Hotel for a cup of fresh brewed Ceylon tea. If you want to get away from the busy streets of Kandy, take a tuk-tuk to the wonderful Royal Botanical Gardens. It is tranquil and very beautiful to stroll around.

KANDY – THE CULTURAL HUB

The gateway to historical sites

Kandy is not only a main rail hub, it is also the gateway to both historical sites and Sri Lanka's Hill Country. Here you can enjoy hiking at Adam's Peak, or visit the tea factories and plantations.

Kandy has a rich history and cultural past. The UNESCO world heritage site has historically had a higher cultural importance than Colombo, as for centuries it was its own Kingdom. Kandy boasts the beautiful Royal Botanical Gardens, a university and on Sri Lanka's most famous site, the Temple of the Tooth – a Buddhist Temple where the sacred relic of Buddha's tooth is kept. The Kingdom of Kandy lasted between the 15th century to the early 19th century. In 1815 the Kingdom of Kandy became a part of the British Empire following the Kandyan Convention.

Kandy's climate is a bit cooler and more temperate in comparison with the Colombo heat, as the ancient city sits at a higher altitude, with hills surrounding the city.

Take a stroll by the lake and pass by the Temple of the Tooth.

TEMPLE OF THE TOOTH/ SRI DALADA MALIGAWA

Sri Dalada Veediya, Kandy

The Temple of the Tooth holds the relic of the tooth of Buddha. As a famous pilgrimage site, welcoming Buddhists from around the world, it was therefore very symbolic when three suicide bombers from the militant organisation Liberation Tigers of Tamil Eelam (LTTE) killed themselves in attack on the Temple in 1998. They crashed their truck through the temple gates, killing many civilians. The attack was just days before the planned celebration activities of 50 years of independence from Great Britain – the 50th Independence Day.

It is a beautiful experience to enter this place of worship, which is filled with flowers and shining Buddhist artwork. Every day certain rituals are performed around the sacred shrine of the relic. The tooth is not visible, as it is kept in the smallest of seven golden caskets. Before the attack, the tooth left the temple once a year during a 10-day parade called Esala Perahera, which is celebrated with elephants, dancers, fire-breathers and drummers. Now the festival continues without the relic, but it is still one of the grandest of all Sri Lanka's Buddhist festivals and remains closely connected to the Temple of the Tooth. It is held in July or August each year.

HIGH TEA AT QUEEN'S HOTEL

D S Senanayake Veediya, Kandy

One of Sri Lanka's oldest hotels, with a heritage of over 160 years, the hotel is located right opposite the temple and offers great views of Kandy Lake. The hotel has a true colonial-era ambience. Built in 1841 as a colonial residence, Queen's Hotel was formerly the residence of the Governor of Ceylon.

A nod to its history, the hotel's bar, The Pub Royal takes you right back to the days of British rule, and the Lord Mountbatten Lounge Bar was named after the famous commander, who was a frequent guest during his time in Kandy. If walking around the lake has given you an appetite, the hotel also serves high tea.

KANDY'S ROYAL BOTANICAL GARDENS

Peradeniya Road, Kandy

Upon arriving at Kandy by train, you can easily take a tuk-tuk to the Royal Botanical Gardens, as it is just a 10–15 minute drive from the railway station. I highly recommend a visit to the gardens, as they are beautiful and very exotic. You can easily spend half a day there, walking around the fantastic small botanical worlds and discovering exotic and unique plants and trees that you most probably have never seen before. There is also an orchid house inside the gardens. Sri Lanka has 188 species of wild orchid, with more than half of them originating from the Kandy region.

TRUE BEAUTY

My favourite trees are the cannonball tree with its fantastic flowers in wax-orange and pink and its big cannonball like fruits, the gigantic palm trees and the java fig with its beautiful playful, crooked branches.

The famous Java fig trees invite you to sit on their curvy branches, or for children to climb them.

The Royal Palm Avenue with its impressive symmetry.

Majestic palm tree. There are over 200 species of palms in the gardens.

ROYAL ROOTS

The origins of the gardens date back to 1371 when the Sinhalese King Wickramabahu III set up his royal court by the Mahaweli River.

The Royal Botanical Gardens was established around 1780 by King Kirti Sri. After the takeover of the British, the famous botanist Sir Joseph Banks set up the Royal Botanical Gardens in Kew outside London. Under his advice, an outpost of Kew Gardens was opened first in Slave Island in Colombo and then relocated to Kandy and Peradeniya in 1843. The purpose of the gardens was to enable the collection and study of tropical plant species and their seeds and to send their samples and findings back to Kew Gardens.

Many monarchs and politicians have visited the gardens and planted trees as a symbolic gesture. A big Ceylon ironwood tree was planted by the last Russian Tsar, Nicholas II, in 1894 and a cannonball tree was planted in 1901 by King George V and Queen Mary of the United Kingdom. Other luminaries, such as Indira Gandhi and the Soviet cosmonaut Yuri Gagarin have also planted trees in the gardens.

A Buddhist monk with his apprentices, walking and learning.

INTERNATIONAL APPEAL

The park receives visitors from all corners of the world. As well as international visitors, the gardens also attract Sri Lankans from all walks of life, from students and Buddhist monks, to families with children and couples strolling hand-in-hand.

A walk in the gardens is cool and enjoyable thanks to the trees, which provide plenty of shade. You can take lunch at one of the gardens' restaurants or bring you own picnic and sit calmly while enjoying the fantastic environment of the gardens.

The trees are homes to flying foxes who dangle overhead.

GREEN GOLD – TEA PLANTATIONS

The green gold of Sri Lanka – It is here where Ceylon tea is produced. On these beautiful green slopes, the tea leaves are picked by mostly women, wearing saris, walking up and down the hills.

Most of the workers in Sri Lanka's tea industry are Tamils, who came to Sri Lanka in the 1860s from the South of India.

THE TEA PLANT – CAMELLIA SINENSIS

Evergreen leaves

The tea plant, or camellia sinensis, is an evergreen shrub whose leaves and buds can be used to produce tea. Many think that black and green teas come from different plant species. In fact, they come from the same species, the difference being that black tea is fermented.

FACTS ABOUT CEYLON TEA

HIGH GROWN TEA

Region: Nuwara Eliya, Uda Pussellawa, Uva, Dimbulla
Cultivated at over 1300 m altitude. Mountain grown at low temperatures, light, delicate flavour.

MID GROWN TEA

Region: Kandy
Cultivated at between 600 m and 1300 m altitude.
Copper coloured appearance, full-bodied.

LOW GROWN TEA

Region: Sabaragamuwa, Ruhuna
Cultivated at under 600 m altitude. Grows faster, long leaves.

TEA PROCESS

Plucking, withering, rolling, fermenting, drying, sorting and grading, packaging.

HOW TO BREW TEA?

Let the water boil, let the tea steep for 3 to 4 minutes.

GROW YOUR KNOWLEDGE WITH A TEA FACTORY TOUR

When you enter a tea factory, it smells of freshly picked tea leaves. The green leaves, which are hand-picked, are stored in large, long trays. This is where the "withering" takes place. The process of producing tea, from picking to packaging, takes just 24 hours. The processes in between define whether the tea will be black, green, white, caffeinated or decaffeinated. Green tea has not been oxidised.

There are so many factors that have an impact on the taste of tea: the soil, the altitude at which the tea has been grown, the age of the tea leaf and how it is handled in the tea factory. Tea is certainly not just tea. Sri Lanka has 7 tea growing regions: Kandy, Nuwara Eliya, Uda Pussellawa, Uva, Dimbulla, Sabaragamuwa and Ruhuna.

If you visit a tea factory, you will learn more about tea and how it is picked and handled throughout the production process. The old factories usually look like relics of Victorian industry and are often built in the same style; white barns located very close to the tea plantations. The factories were constructed in England, then shipped over in pieces.

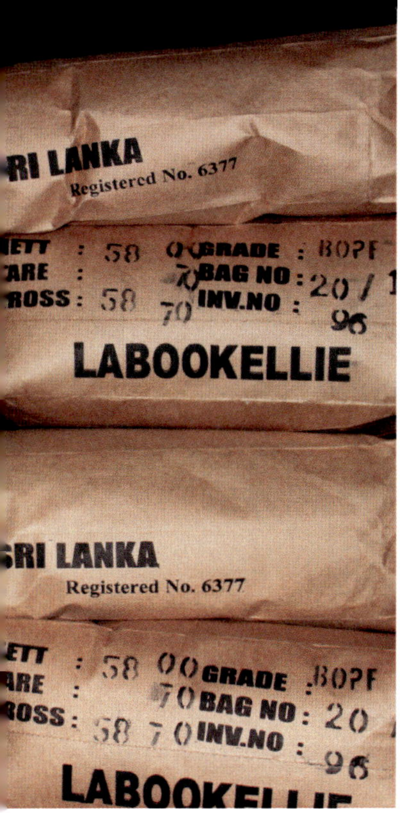

THE HEART OF CEYLON'S TEA UNIVERSE

Once you have witnessed the art of tea production – from the fresh leaves picked from the green hills and stored to wither, to the final boxed batches – to drink a cup of Ceylon tea feels even more precious. To sit and enjoy it in the heart of Sri Lanka's Ceylon tea district makes it all the more tastier.

TEA GROWING AREAS IN SRI LANKA

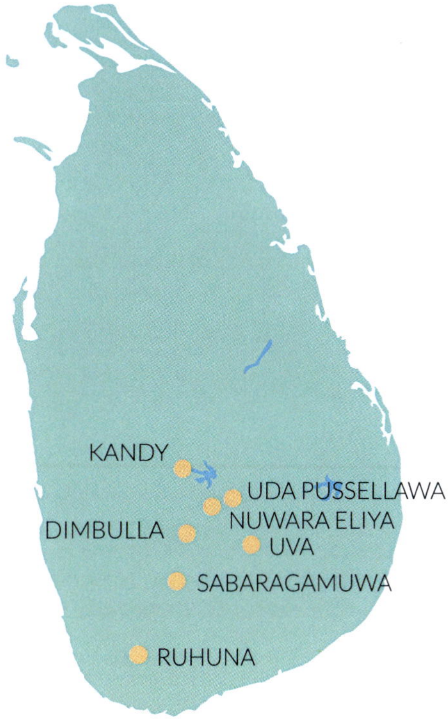

NUWARA ELIYA – LITTLE ENGLAND

Here the British can feel at home, as they did when they arrived in the 19th century. The climate is much closer to a British summer than to Colombo's. Often foggy and misty, during daytime it is around 20 degrees, while at night the temperature can go down to 10 degrees Celsius. Here in the hill country the wealthy people of Colombo have their retreats, where they come to escape the heat and dust of the capital. The city of Nuwara Eliya has been called Little England.

GRAND HOTEL IN NUWARA ELIYA

5 Grand Hotel Rd, Nuwara Eliya 22200, Sri Lanka

Grand Hotel in Nuwara Eliya is a very British looking, flamboyant hotel housed in an Elizabethan style manor house. Built in 1891, the 154 room hotel was the mansion of the former Governor of Sri Lanka, Sir Edward Barnes. As you enter, the hotel lives up to its name, as there is a very grand feeling to it. If a colonial era experience is what you're after, this hotel offers plenty of it. The service, food and rooms meet the highest expectations. In fact, Queen Elizabeth II even stopped by for a cup of tea on Easter Sunday, back in 1954.

RAMBODA FALLS – A BEAUTIFUL 100 METRE WATERFALL

A5, Ramboda, Sri Lanka

Sri Lanka has around 350 waterfalls. One of them is Ramboda Falls, which measures 109 metres in height. The nature surrounding the waterfall is very beautiful, with lots of impressive Bougainvillea flowers. It is a wonderful place to stop for lunch or a break and enjoy the beauty.

SIGIRIYA – LION ROCK

Climbing among Sri Lanka's ancient past and the wonderful, natural setting of Sigiriya. The great view, giant lion claws, the gardens and the sweet monkeys watching our steps.

Sigiriya is an ancient rock fortress, located between the towns of Dambulla and Habarana, in the central province of Sri Lanka.

THE EIGHTH WONDER OF THE WORLD

This natural landmark has an interesting history from being a kingdom, to becoming a Buddhist monastery. King Kasyapa had a great vision when he initiated this fantastic project; to build a fortress, a palace and a small kingdom up on a rock, in the design of a lion.

MAGMA FROM AN EXTINCT VOLCANO

Sigiriya rock's plateau is formed from magma of an extinct volcano. At almost 200 metres high, the rock stands out against the landscape of the surrounding plains and forests.

THE KINGDOM OF KASYAPA

King Kasyapa chose the rock as the site for his palace in the 5th Century. Although not the easiest spot to access, elegant pavilions, pools and gardens were created. Kasyapa was the son of King Dhatusena of Anuradhapura, but as he was not destined to inherit the crown, he left the capital to create a new city and establish his own Kingdom at Sigiriya.

EARLY ROCK PORTRAITS FROM THE 5TH CENTURY

The ancient rock palace has some very unique and well-preserved frescoes, with portraits of b are-breasted, beautiful women. No one really knows who these ladies were. Most probably they were females of the court; concubines, dancers, servants, or even possibly princesses. It's quite unique that they are still visible after more than 1,500 years. The organic pigments have survived both UV rays from the sunlight and from being overpainted or destroyed at the hands of humans.

Fast facts

- *Pronounced: See-gee-RI-yah*
- *UNESCO declared Sigiriya a World Heritage site in 1982*
- *The term Sigiriya originates from the word Sinhagiri i.e. Lion Rock*
- *King Kasyapa built a palace on the top of the rock in the 5th century*

WALL OF REFLECTION

Upon climbing the stairs of the rock, you pass the Mirror Wall. It's a polished part of the rock and it is said that in the old days, it was polished so thoroughly that the king could see his reflection in it. The Mirror Wall is filled with inscriptions and poems written by visitors to Sigiriya. The most ancient inscriptions are dated from the 7th–8th century.

THE BEAUTIFUL GARDENS OF THE ROCK

Monks lived in the caves of the rock from as early as the 3rd century BC. After Kasyapa's death at the end of the 5th century, the rock was taken over by Buddhist monks, with a monastery there until the 14th century, when it was abandoned.

The gardens of Sigiriya are among the oldest landscaped gardens in the world. There are different types of gardens, from water, cave and boulder gardens, to terraced sections.

ARRIVE EARLY

It's good to be an early bird and begin climbing Sigiriya's rock as soon as it opens in the morning, as around noon it gets really hot, especially at the plateau of the rock, when the sun stands in its zenith. Don't forget to bring drinking water, a hat, and good walking shoes.

DO I DARE TO CLIMB THE ROCK?

You might ask yourself – "Do I dare to climb the stairs?" Is the sun too hot, or are the stairs too steep? The answer is, you can probably make it, but don't look down too much as you climb the final stairs to the top. You can also choose to stop by the giant lion's claws if it becomes too much. People can be seen taking care of each other on the way up, holding hands, with some walking very slowly, but in general, most people can manage the one hour walk up the rock. Children can also climb the rock, but I think a good age is around 8 years and up. There are places if you need to take a break during the climb, which is fun because this will give you the chance to get to know a couple of monkeys as you watch the view.

WATCH THE SUN RISE AND SET OVER SIGIRIYA

Another tip is to climb the nearby Pidurangala Rock to see the sunrise or sunset over Sigiriya. If you start very early in the morning (around 5 AM) you can see the first rays of sun spreading over the landscape – a totally breathtaking view. Sigiriya is bathed in a warm, golden light before sunset, creating an almost spiritual moment.

"What is the best thing about Sigiriya Rock?" I asked my 8 year-old son. "The great view and the giant lion claws" was his answer. He was the first of us to reach the top of the rock.

PINNAWALA ELEPHANT ORPHANAGE

B199, Rambukkana 71100, near the town of Kegalle

Elephants are majestic, loving creatures and an important part of Sri Lanka. When visiting Sri Lanka, it's a great experience to get close to the elephants, and there are many different wildlife parks to visit. The Pinnawala Elephant Orphanage is totally dedicated to elephants. You can see elephants of different ages, sizes and with different personalities and stories. It's a true joy to see how they enjoy bathing and playing in the river.

Elephant facts

- *Maximum age: 80 years. Average life expectancy is 40 – 60 years old*
- *Weight: up to 6 tons*
- *Elephants can cry, smile and are loving creatures that mourn their dead for days*
- *Communicating at a lower frequency than us, they communicate a lot through their feet and the ground*
- *Elephants can suffer from sunburn. They protect themselves by throwing sand on their skin*
- *They drink 150 litres of water per day*

CARING FOR BABY ELEPHANTS

Sri Lanka has about 5,500 wild elephants on the island. It's an amazing number of elephants. The Pinnawala Elephant Orphanage was founded in 1975 by the Sri Lanka Department of Wildlife Conservation, with the purpose of taking care of young baby elephants when, for example, the mother had been killed. During the war, elephants were hurt in different ways as part of the conflict and there have been several accidents where elephants have walked on a landmine. These elephants found a place in Pinnawala. The orphanage is situated northeast of the town of Kegalle, halfway between Colombo and Kandy in the hills of central Sri Lanka.

THE HERD IS COMING – IT'S FEEDING TIME

A great stretch of land has been assigned to the Pinnawala Elephant Orphanage and the elephants can move freely in a herd within the area. They are fed at certain hours, which is when you as a visitor can see them. Newborn baby elephants are fed with feeding bottles and around 3 times per day visitors can participate in the feeding.

BATHING AND DRINKING AT THE RIVER

After feeding time, it is time for the elephants to head to the river to drink some of the 150 litres of water that they need each day. They also take a bath and play with each other in the water.

The daily routine

- *08.00 The babies are fed milk in the mornings and are allowed to run freely on the 12 acres of grassland*
- *At 10.00 and 14.00 each day the animals are walked to the river Maha Oya for a two-hour bath*
- *The elephants are fed mainly coconut leaves (Cocos nucifera), jackfruit branches (Artocarpus integra) and leaves*

Source: Pinnawala Elephant Orphanage website

SOUTH OF COLOMBO

Visit Galle Fort the 16th century site that withstood the tsunami • Shop for local fashion and hand crafts • Discover the island's pristine beaches • Go on safari on land or sea

ENJOY COLONIAL HERITAGE WITH A HIP FLAVOUR

Galle Fort

Galle Fort is a charming and beautifully preserved colonial-era fortified town. It is one of Sri Lanka's prime attractions and a UNESCO world heritage site, and it is easy to understand why. It is unique in so many different ways. I have returned many times, as I just love to walk around and take in the history of the preserved colonial buildings along its streets. Galle Fort is filled with architectural gems and boutiques set against the backdrop of normal Sri Lankan life, with children swimming in the ocean or going home from school in the fort.

Galle Fort has a rich, diverse history. Under a succession of colonial rule, each power left its own mark, creating a historical and architectural mash-up that makes it unique. The Portuguese landed in Galle in the 16th century and built a fort. Galle was then captured from the Portuguese by the Dutch in 1640, with a force led by the first Dutch Governor of Ceylon, Willem Jacobszoon Coster. The Dutch fortified Galle during the 17th century and built the strong walls upon which it is possible to take a pleasant stroll around the fort. In 1796 the British era began as they took over – just a week after they captured Colombo.

STANDING UP TO THE TSUNAMI

The strong, Dutch-built walls surrounding the fort withstood the Boxing Day Tsunami in 2004. The tsunami hit the Sri Lankan eastern coast almost an hour before reaching the west coast and Galle. The city of Galle outside of the fort area and the south coast villages were strongly hit, with houses and people swept away. In the Galle area alone, several thousands of people died.

A WALK IN THE FORT

Take a walk inside the walls of Galle Fort. See the Galle Lighthouse, the clock tower and for a view of the ocean, walk along the top of the walls of the fort. Along the streets you can find romantic Dutch colonial houses, some of which have remained under the ownership of Dutch families for hundreds of years.

Groote Kerk the Dutch Reformed Church is Sri Lanka's oldest protestant church. Built in 1755, it was constructed on the site of a Portuguese Capuchin convent. Inside the church and in the cemetery, ancient gravestones pave the floor. Many men who left Holland and never returned are buried within the Fort.

In Court Square you can find several old administrative buildings, the court, law firms and administrative buildings. It is also the perfect spot to rest for a while under the fantastic banyan trees.

LUNCH AT AMANGALLA HOTEL

10 Church Street, Galle 80000

Amangalla Hotel is the perfect place to enjoy lunch in the spirit of the 19th century. The hotel was formerly known as the New Oriental Hotel and was the stop for passengers travelling on P&O Steamers. Inside, the hotel is filled with original antiques and wonderful 300 year-old teak floors, while outside on the hotel's shaded veranda, staff serve lunch or high tea in the afternoon.

A BREAK AT THE FORT PRINTERS

39 Pedlar Street, Galle Fort, Galle

The Fort Printers is a small boutique hotel with just a few rooms and a lovely restaurant. The building dates back to the 18th century. Built as a mansion, it later became the home of a traditional printing facility, hence the name.

The Fort Printers has a beautiful shady courtyard. It is the perfect place to sit and enjoy the ambience and escape the heat of the fort. You may even be greeted by a Galle Fort monkey as it climbs over the roofs.

The menus are beautifully decorated with the fragrant flowers of the Frangipani tree, otherwise known as Temple Flowers. It is the perfect spot to enjoy breakfast, a meal, afternoon tea or just a fresh mango juice.

BOUTIQUE SHOPPING FOR ANTIQUES OR FURNITURE

Galle Fort is more than history and good food. Many of the old houses along the narrow streets have been converted into small boutiques. The shops offer a great selection, with a focus on ethical and ecological products. Here you can find gems, jewellery, clothes, antiques, Sri Lankan crafts and spa and Ayurveda products.

For luxury Ayurveda spa products and treatments, visit the concept store of the global luxury Ayurveda chain, Spa Ceylon. For beautiful locally produced fabrics, clothes, gifts and art, Barefoot has a large boutique here. Rejecting the factory system, Barefoot products are either crafted in private homes predominantly by women, or in small workshops by local craftsmen.

Another great boutique is The Three by TPV, which sells clothes, home décor and hand crafted items. Products are designed and made by local craftsmen in a range of natural materials, including wood and stone.

If you have an interest in colonial antiques and traditional Sri Lankan furniture, Olanda Furniture in Galle Fort sells a large selection of wooden furniture in the traditional Sri Lankan style.

DRINKS AT GALLE FORT HOTEL

28 Church Street, Galle Fort, Galle

Galle Fort Hotel was originally a 17th century Dutch mansion. A regency top floor was added during the British era, but then the building fell into disrepair. In 1999 the building was purchased and renovated into a boutique hotel.

The 18th century doors and windows on the building's façade are unique within the Fort and in the centre of the hotel is a beautiful colonnaded courtyard with a pool and a garden flush with blossom. In 2007 UNESCO awarded the hotel the Pacific Heritage Award of Distinction as a masterpiece of cultural heritage and conservation. The hotel has just 12 rooms, so if you don't manage to stay there, it's a wonderful place to go in the evening for drinks. With its whirling ceiling fans, soft brown colour scheme and the beautiful courtyard surrounding the pool – the only things missing are Ingrid Bergman and Humphrey Bogart.

WELCOME TO PARADISE

South coast beaches

The south coast beaches are paradisiacal. Lined with beautiful palm trees and with fine, white-golden sand they are very exotic. Nearby are interesting sites like Galle Fort and jungles filled with impressive wildlife. There are many beaches along the south coast, but I have chosen my two favourites: Unawatuna Beach and Mirissa Beach.

UNAWATUNA BEACH

Close to Galle Fort

Just 10 minutes away from Galle Fort in a tuk-tuk, Unawatuna is one of Sri Lanka's most famous beaches. This small coastal town has a beautiful beach with golden sand, turquoise water and many palm trees. When the sun sets in Unawatuna, the entire beach is bathed in a shimmering golden light.

The beach has plenty of wildlife and if you are lucky, you may spot turtles laying eggs along the shore. Unawatuna is great for bathing, snorkelling and diving because of the double reef over the bay, which creates a natural pool. The average water temperature is around 28°C all year round. If you take a 30-minute boat ride, you can also go on a wreck dive and explore the SS Rangoon, a British steamer which sank 100 years ago. It sits upright on the sea bed, its masts intact.

Unawatuna has a good selection of guesthouses and restaurants along the beach, making it a popular destination among travellers. I suggest a visit to Galle Fort, then stay in a guesthouse in Unawatuna, as the towns are only 6 kilometres apart.

MIRISSA BEACH

A coastal gem

Smaller than Unawatuna Beach, Mirissa has one of the most beautiful south coast beaches. Mirissa is a coastal village between the larger cities, Galle and Matara. It has a nice calm atmosphere. It is easy to relax under the palm trees and just listen to the sound of the waves in the Indian Ocean. Early in the morning Yoga classes are held at the beach and it is pleasant to walk along the beach when the sand is still cold under foot.

Mirissa is the perfect spot for enjoying Sri Lanka's south coast beach life, with good seafood and drinks. Mirissa is the largest fishing port on the south coast, so lots of good fish, such as: lobster, tuna, mullet, snapper and butterfish reach the restaurants every day. Mirissa is also a small surfers paradise for both beginners and more advanced surfers. Finally, it is also known for its unique Blue Whale Safari.

BLUE WHALE WATCHING

Mirissa is famous for its blue whale watching. Blue whales are by far the largest animals on earth. Measuring around 30 metres long and weighing approximately 140 tonnes, they are quite outstanding. They are bigger than the largest dinosaurs were. The whale watching season in Sri Lanka runs between November to April and apart from blue whales, you may also spot a number of dolphins during the safari. In Sri Lanka there are three places offering blue whale safaris: Mirissa, Kalpitiya in the Puttalam District and Trincomalee on the east coast. The waves can be quite big during the safari, so if you suffer from sea sickness, it may be useful to take motion sickness medicine an hour before departure. Don't forget to take your sunglasses and binoculars.

AYURVEDA TREATMENTS

Ayurveda is a holistic approach to health and has, for thousands of years, been used and developed in Sri Lanka. The treatment involves the use of herbs, plants and oils to cure and revitalise the body. Ayurvedic

treatments are available all over Sri Lanka. Many people travel here just for the sake of Ayurveda and spa treatments for the relief of stress and anxiety.

There are many different retreats along the coasts of Sri Lanka and almost every one of the more fashionable hotels offer quality Ayurveda treatments, from massages and facials, to more complicated treatments like Karna Purana (pouring warm oil into the ears), performed by certified staff.

Ayurveda

Ayurveda means the science of life in Sanskrit.

Ayur = life and longevity Veda = knowledge and science

VAST BEACHES AND BOUTIQUE HOTELS

Bentota

Bentota is situated in between Colombo and Galle. We are 65 kilometres south of Colombo and 50 kilometres north of the city of Galle in the Southern Province. Bentota Beach, the supply of both boutique and luxury hotels and the relative closeness to Colombo make it a popular destination and honeymoon spot.

The beach is wide and long stretching, and the sand is clean, soft and white. There is lots of space for taking long walks to just enjoy the beach, nature and sunrise or sunset. In the warm water in Bentota, you can also snorkel or go scuba diving.

A couple of architect Geoffrey Bawa's early built hotels are also to be found in Bentota. Bawa's Bentota Beach Hotel was built in the late 1960s, and is an example of tropical modernism. The hotel has a unique location, between two beaches. It lies on a narrow strip of land between the Bentota River and the Indian Ocean. Other Bawa designed hotels in Bentota are Villa Bentota and Club Villa.

The Bentota River and the mangrove swamps are rich in wildlife, with crocodiles, varanes, lizards and birds. If you are interested in fishing, you can go deep sea fishing or lagoon fishing. The best is to go early in the morning if you want to succeed in catching something.

CROCODILES IN THE MANGROVE SWAMP

It is a beautiful experience to take a small boat through the mangrove swamps of Bentota River. A greenish, golden sunlight shines through the leaves of the mangrove trees, their tree tops reflected in the water. Lians - the mangrove's root system - bind the trees together in a tight vegetation. As the boat sweeps silently through the water with its engine turned off, suddenly the guide shows you that the log in the water in front of you isn't a log – it is a crocodile! With so many crocs in the swamp, you may not be too keen to take a dip in the water.

As part of the Bentota River Safari, you can stop and cuddle a baby crocodile.

Even though they are quite small, the eyes of the baby crocodile give a sharp glare. Its stare, combined with those small, sharp teeth are certainly worthy of respect, even at such a young age.

TRAVELLING TO YALA

A wildlife haven, full of natural beauty

Yala is situated in the south east part of the Island, about 10 hours' drive from Colombo, so I recommend an overnight stop along the way. You can find plenty of nice hotels in one of the lovely south coast beach towns along the way, or stay near the park so that you can get there early in the morning.

Yala National Park is one of Sri Lanka's largest national parks. It was designated as a wildlife sanctuary by the British in 1900, then became a national park in 1938. Yala is most famous for its leopards, but it is also the home to a great number of other animals like crocodiles, buffaloes, monkeys, elephants and a great variety of birds.

The nature and landscape is beautiful and varies from grassy plains and light forests, to lagoons with lotus flowers. It continues out to the Indian Ocean, where you can enjoy its totally pristine, lovely white sand beaches. Here you can stop for a fruit break and stretch your legs during a jeep ride, or just enjoy the ocean.

EARLY MORNING JEEP SAFARI

Up before sunrise

The best time for visiting Yala National Park is early in the morning. It is nice and cool, and the park is calm and peaceful as the sun rises with a soft rose-gold light washing over the landscape. If you have booked a jeep safari in advance, the jeep driver will pick you up from your hotel at five o'clock in the morning, when it is still dark, and take you to the park. Here, the other jeeps taking the morning safari are lined up ready to drive into the park when it opens at 6 AM.

Yala's most famous animal is the leopard. However, although the leopard is heavily promoted, you are not so likely to spot any leopards during the safari. You will more likely see elephants taking a bath in a lotus covered lagoon, water-buffaloes grazing on grass, or stunning peacocks walking beside the roads. These animals are more used to the jeeps and are not bothered by their interruption. Only one fifth of the park is open for jeep safaris; the rest of the park is closed to visitors and is dedicated to the wellbeing and preservation of the wildlife.

UP IN THE ECO TREE HOUSE

Yala Eco Tree House, Tissamaharama 82600

Almost as exciting as going to the Yala National Park is to spend a night in the nearby Eco Tree House.

The balcony is high up in the tree, so the view is fantastic. It is a great place to sit and read a good book, or just watch the fields and forest on the horizon. The peacocks stroll back and forth below, making funny noises, but they pay no attention to you as you sit high up in the tree.

The Eco Tree House has big windows, so you can lie in bed and connect with the nature outside and watch the sunrise.

All the different sounds from the tree make you feel like a part of the tree's own eco-community. It also allows you to watch your bird neighbours at a very close distance. It will probably also be the first time that you have taken a shower up in a tree.

In the evening, dinner is served after sunset. The small path from the tree house to the little house where you will dine is lit with a row of candles. The darkness around the tree is massive and you will feel that you are far away from everything and in the middle of something special.

The tree, the nature surrounding the tree, the animals and the different sounds merge into one great experience. To spend a couple of nights in a Sri Lankan tree is something you will never forget.

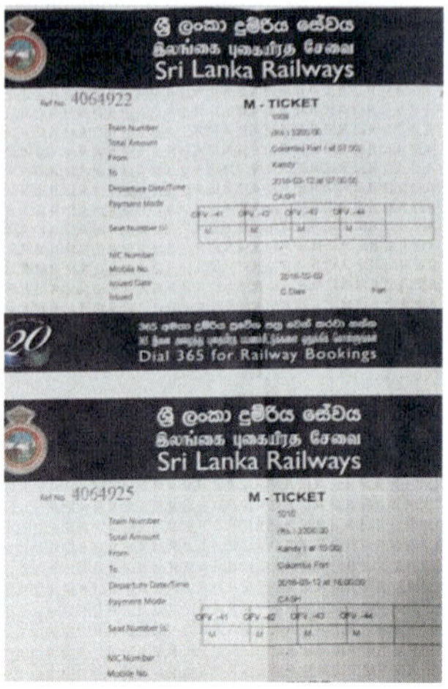
ශ්‍රී ලංකා දුම්රිය සේවය
இலங்கை புகையிரத சேவை
Sri Lanka Railways
4064922
M - TICKET
Dial 365 for Railway Bookings
ශ්‍රී ලංකා දුම්රිය සේවය
இலங்கை புகையிரத சேவை
Sri Lanka Railways
4064925
M - TICKET

3698

PRACTICAL ADVICE

Tips for travel, hotels and shopping

INTERESTING ADDRESSES AND LINKS

Unique hotels and shopping

COLONIAL HOTELS

COLOMBO

Galle Face Hotel
2 Galle Road, Colombo 03
gallefacehotel.com
+94 11 254 1010

Mount Lavinia Hotel
100 Hotel Road, Mount Lavinia
mountlaviniahotel.com
+94 11 2711711

Paradise Road Tintagel Colombo
65 Rosmead Place, Colombo 07
paradiseroadhotels.com/tintagel
+94 11 460 2060

KANDY

Queen's Hotel
D S Senanayake Veediya, Kandy
20000
queenshotel.lk
+94 81 2233026

NUWARA ELIYA

Grand Hotel
Grand Hotel Rd, Nuwara Eliya 22200,
Sri Lanka
grandhotel.tangerinehotels.com
+94 52 2222881-7

GALLE FORT

The Galle Fort Hotel
28 Church Street, Galle Fort, Galle
galleforthotel.com
+94 76 665 8080

The Fort Printers
39 Pedlar Street, Galle Fort, Galle
thefortprinters.com
+94 912 247 977

Amangalla (formerly The New Oriental Hotel)
aman.com/resorts/amangalla
10 Church Street
Galle 80000
+94 912 233 388

HOTELS BY ARCHITECT GEOFFREY BAWA

The Blue Water Hotel and Spa
Thalpitiya, Wadduwa
bluewatersrilanka.com
+94 38 2235067-8

Jetwing Lighthouse
433 A Dadella, Galle
jetwinghotels.com/jetwinglighthouse
+94 114 709 400

Club Bentota
Paradise Island, Aluthgama
clubbentota.com
+94 342 275 167

Bentota Beach by Cinnamon
Galle Rd, Bentota, 80500
bentota-beach-by-cinnamon-bentota-sri-lanka.en.www.lk
+94 342 275 176

Paradise Road The Villa Bentota
138/18 - 138/22 Galle Road, 80500 Bentota
paradiseroadhotels.com
+94 34 227 5311

Club Villa Bentota
138/15 Galle Road, Bentota
clubvillabentota.com
+94 34 22 75312

SHOPPING IN COLOMBO & GALLE FORT

COLOMBO

Kala Pola Art Market
Ananda Coomaraswamy Mawatha, Colombo 07

Racecourse Promenade shopping mall
Reid Avenue, Colombo 07

Arcade – Independence Square
Independence Square, Colombo 07

The Dutch Hospital
Hospital St, Colombo 01

Spa Ceylon
103/7 Galle Road, Colombo 03
spaceylon.com

Barefoot
704 Galle Road, Colombo 03
barefootceylon.com

GALLE FORT

The Three by TPV
43 Layn Baan Street, Fort Galle 80000
thethreebytpv.com

Paradise Road Flagship store
213 Dharmapala Mawatha, Colombo 07
paradiseroad.lk/shops

Olanda Furniture
30 Leyn Baan Street, Fort, Galle
olandafurniture.com

FLYING TO SRI LANKA

Sri Lanka has three airports: Ratmalana Airport, Mattala Rajapaksa International Airport and Bandaranaike International Airport, which is Sri Lanka's main airport. Bandaranaike Airport is located 30 kilometres north of Colombo. The country's national airline, SriLankan Airlines, along with a number of airlines including: Emirates Airlines, Cathay Pacific, Qantas, KLM and Thai Airways, fly from Sri Lanka to a number of destinations worldwide.

APPLYING FOR A VISA

A visa, or ETA (Electronic Travel Authorisation) is required to visit Sri Lanka and must be obtained prior to arrival. Tourist visas are valid for 30 days from the date of entry. However, for longer stays, it is possible to obtain a six-month visa.

For more information or to apply online, visit:
eta.gov.lk/slvisa/

BY TRAIN

Travelling by train in Sri Lanka is both exciting and affordable. The stretch between Ella and Colombo takes about seven hours and is said to be the world's most beautiful train route. As it winds around verdant mountains and past tea plantations, the colours are like nothing you've ever seen. Sri Lanka's railway system was built by the British in 1864 as a means of transporting tea and coffee from the Hill county to Colombo. Taking the train is like taking a journey back in time.

It is easy to take a day trip from Colombo to Kandy and back, if you start early in the morning. You can see the train timetables on Sri Lanka Railway's website. It is wise to purchase your ticket a day or two in advance as the trains are usually full.

railway.gov.lk

BY TAXI

For travelling by taxi around Colombo, Kangaroo Cabs provides a good, reliable service. You can book cabs for airport pickup, van deliveries and even weddings! Bookings can be made online, by phone, or if you travel frequently by cab, it may be worth downloading the Kangaroo Cabs app.

Kangaroo Cabs
+94 11 2 588588
2588588.com

TUK-TUK

For smaller trips, tuk-tuks are a fun way to travel. Tuk-tuk trips in Colombo start at 50 rupees, and cost around 200–500 rupees for a typical journey.

SOURCES AND FURTHER READING

GEOFFREY BAWA AND HIS ARCHITECTURE

archdaily.com, Spotlight Geoffrey Bawa, 23 July, 2018

archnet.org, authorities: Geoffrey Bawa

At Home in Sri Lanka, James Fennel and Tom Sykes, 2016

geoffreybawa.com

Geoffrey Bawa: The Complete Works, David Robson, 2002

lanka.com, People: Geoffrey Bawa

The New Sri Lankan Houses, David Robson, Robert Powell, Sebastian Posingis, 2015

SRI LANKA'S LEGACY

BBC News: *Sri Lanka's famous Galle Face Hotel doorman dies*, November, 2014

CNN World News: *8 killed in Sri Lankan blast at temple*, Jan 1998

Financial Times: *How empire and disaster shaped Sri Lanka's botanical gardens*, Feb 2016

Huffington Post: *The Truth About Where Cinnamon Comes From*, March 2014

Lonely Planet: Nuwara Eliya, 2018

New York Times: *11 Killed in Truck Bombing at Sri Lanka Buddhist Site*, 1998

Scotland is now: *Scotland's legacy in Sri Lanka*, April 2015

Sunday Observer: *Cargills – over 150 years in business and still going strong*, Jan 2012

Sunday Observer: *Dutch Reformed Church of Galle: Dutch period's finest monument*, June 2017

The Guardian: *Gentle touch*, Dec 2013

The Times: *Sri Lanka: an island paradise*, October 2012

Time Out: *Colonial Buildings of Nuwara Eliya*, March 2015

UK Essays: *Pearl of the Indian Ocean, An Overview of Sri Lanka*, June 2017

Yamu.lk: General Post Office

Yamu.lk Central Point – The Economic History Museum of Sri Lanka

NATURE

Botanical Gardens – kew.org

Elephants – nationalgeographic.com

Kandy Botanical Gardens – botanicgardens.gov.lk

Pinnawala Elephant Orphanage – nationalzoo.gov.lk

Unawatuna – divebooker.com

Whale watching – whale-watching-mirissa.com

Yala National Park – yalasrilanka.lk

TOURISM

bestoflanka.com

ceylonrusticguide.com

dreamofacity.com

exploresrilanka.lk

insightguides.com

lanka.com

lonelyplanet.com

sigiriyatourism.com

Sri Lanka Tourism –

srilanka.travel

Temple of the Sacred Tooth, sridaladamaligawa.lk

theculturetrip.com

thesrilankandream.co.uk

visitcolombo.com

TEA

ceylonblacktea.com

dilmahtea.com

Plants of the World online: Camellia sinensis

Pure Ceylon Tea: Tea Growing Regions

Regions, pureceylontea.com

Sri Lanka Tea Board: Annual Report, 2017

twinings.co.uk

FACTS

Etymology Dictionary: Sri Lanka, etymoline.com

Sri Lanka, Britannica.com

unesco.org

wikipedia.com

wwf.org

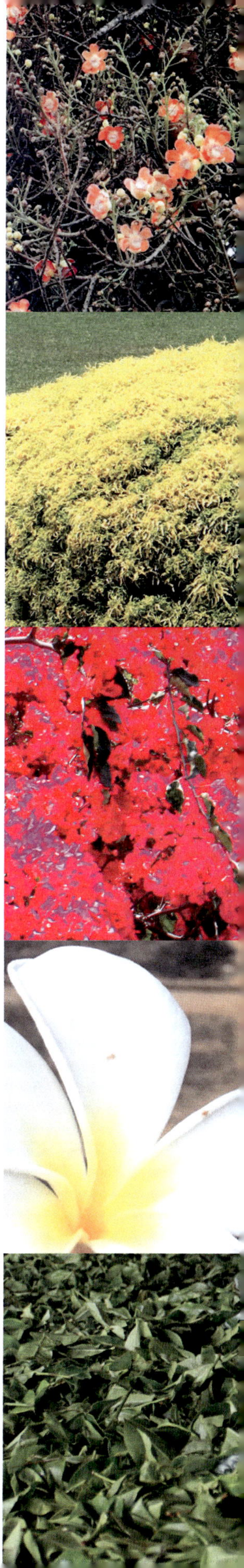

INDEX

ACKNOWLEDGEMENTS

Thanks to all the Sri Lankans I have met during my travels, for being so warm-hearted and sharing in every possible way. Thanks also to my lovely family, my fantastic colleagues at Adentity and my dear friends in Berlin for your encouragement, support and for making this book possible.

INFO

First published: November, 2018
Original title: Explore the Beauty of Sri Lanka – Heritage, Culture and Nature
Language: English

Publisher: Adentity, Sweden
Photography & Text: Lina Nicander
Layout & illustrations: Mia Borstrand
Editing: Ashlee Beard
ISBN: 978-91-527-9998-7

beautyofsrilanka.com

Photo: Fredrik Birkler

ABOUT THE AUTHOR

Lina Nicander is a passionate traveller with a great interest in languages, culture, nature and history. She has a great love for photography and sharing knowledge, experiences and stories. She is the founder and co-partner of a successful advertising, marketing and communications agency in Sweden. Since 2011 Lina and her family have spent a lot of time visiting, living and working in the Sri Lankan capital and continue to divide their time between Colombo and Malmö.

Made in the USA
Las Vegas, NV
16 December 2024

083d8eed-e3e4-4c36-be68-542f86296351R01